CONTENTS

KT-367-862

SKILLS

.: Starting up :.

It is important to know how to turn your computer on and off safely because this is when it is most likely to go wrong. If your computer crashes, turn it back on again and it should be all right. Once the computer is powered up, Windows will start automatically. It will either go straight to your desktop or, if there are a number of people who use your computer, it will go to the log on screen.

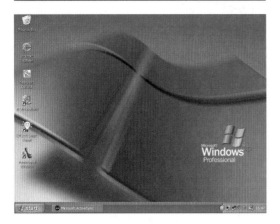

.: Password :.

Click on your user name and you will go to the desktop. If you are using a networked computer or if you have set one up, you might have to add a password to begin.

.: Shutting down :.

When turning off the computer, it is not a good idea to switch off the machine by the power switch or by the socket as this can cause problems. It is better to shut down the PC properly. Log off first, then shut down the machine. It should power off automatically.

If you want to start the computer again immediately, because there was a problem or because you have just installed some software, you can use the **Restart** option. This will shut down the PC automatically, and then turn it on again.

💡 PC MASTER TIP

Most new computers will shut down automatically when you press the power button. To check that this is happening, look for the **Windows is shutting down** phrase on the screen as you turn the computer off.

0100100101011010010100101011010010101010101101010101101100001010

 ## SKILL IN ACTION

Cassie the Cook turns on her PC every morning and turns it off every night. She turns the computer on at the power switch and it starts automatically. The screen appears with a list of users. She clicks on her name to get up the desktop that she uses.

At the end of the morning, she logs off the computer but leaves it turned on in case any of the other staff want to use it while she is at lunch.

At the end of the day, she wants to turn off the computer. First she logs off to make sure that her files are saved, then she shuts down the machine. She waits to make sure that it turns off before leaving work.

EXERCISE

Can you log off your computer without turning it off?

SKILLS

.: Switching on :.

Firstly, find the power button on your computer. This is usually on the front of your machine and will normally be labelled **POWER** or have the following symbol:

If this does not turn your computer on, check that it is switched on at the socket. If there is a button at the back of the machine, check that it is switched on.

.: Switching off :.

To turn off your computer, click on the **Start** button and then click on **Turn Off Computer**.

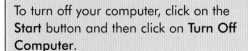

.: Logging off :.

If you want to leave the computer on but need to log off, click on this button instead.

💡 PC MASTER TIP

If you have installed some software and you are asked to restart your computer, you do not need to shut down the machine and then turn it on again. You can use the Restart option instead. This option should appear before you confirm 'shut down'.

PROGRESS CHECK EXERCISE

Can you turn the computer on and off at the socket?

Do you know how to switch users without logging off or turning the computer off?

Can you turn the computer on and off at the power switch?

Do you know how to log on and off the computer?

Can you think of a password to stop other people getting into your work area?

It should not be too obvious and should contain numbers and letters. Remember to change it regularly.

(To set up a password, see page 28.)

Do you know how to make your computer 'sleep' in order to save battery power without logging off?

Some laptops do this if you close the lid.

 # MASTERCLASS

Can you shut down your PC by using the Windows Task Manager, accessed by holding down **Ctrl** and **Alt** then pressing **Delete**?

SKILLS

.: Opening and closing :.

Most of the time you spend at a computer you are using software. You need to open a program first to use it. To save memory, most programs are stored in an unusable form on the hard disk of the computer. They need to be opened into the active area of the computer to work. The more programs you have open in the active area, the slower the computer will run, and the more likely it is to crash.

For this reason, two of the most important skills are opening and closing files. Once files are open, they appear on the screen one at a time unless you make the windows smaller. To go from one file to the next, click on the bottom toolbar on the program that you want.

.: Minimising, maximising :.

A program on this toolbar has been minimised. To maximise it, you can click on it. To minimise an open program, click on the **Minimise** button. The **Restore** button shows the program in a window which you can resize. This can be done by moving the cursor to the edge of the window, clicking the left mouse button and dragging the window to the required size.

Minimise ———  ——— Maximise

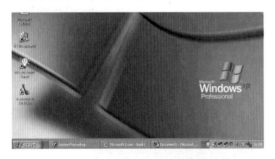

PC MASTER TIP

You can switch between open programs by holding down **Alt** while you click on **Tab**.

01001001010101101001010010101100100101010101101010110110000101

SKILL IN ACTION

Neville the Newsagent needs to open his database program before he can produce lists of deliveries for the paperboys. He has a database that has all the customers' names and addresses and the papers they order. The database is saved in a program called Microsoft® Access. He can open it in a number of ways.

MSACCESS

He does not have an icon for Microsoft® Access on his desktop like the one above so he needs either to find the file or to use the Start button to open the program.

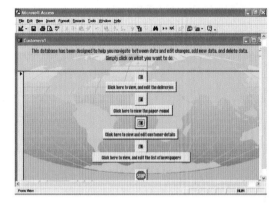

Once he has printed off the lists of deliveries, he needs to close the program. There are two ways that he can do this. He chooses to click on the cross in the top right-hand corner of the window.

EXERCISE

Can you open and close a database application?

THE LATEST NEWS

NEWS FLASH

READ ALL ABOUT IT

SKILLS

.: Opening a file :.

There are a number of ways to open a file. If there is an icon on the desktop, you can simply double click the left-hand mouse button while pointing at the icon. The application will start with a blank document.

 Microsoft Word

.: File icons :.

Move the cursor over the program that you want and click on it.

If you want to open a particular file in the application, you can find the file in the folder that you saved it in. This is often in a **My Documents** folder. The file should have an icon next to it which shows you which application the file will automatically open in.

.: Opening from the Start menu :.

If the application that you want does not have an icon on the desktop, then you need to use the Start menu to find it. Click on the **Start** button in the bottom left-hand corner of the screen. A menu appears and you can click on **All Programs**.

 All Programs

.: Closing a file :.

There are two ways to close a file. Click on **File** on the main menu bar and then **Close**. This will close the file that you are working on but not the application. To close the application you need to click on **File** then **Exit**.

In the top right-hand corner of the window, there are usually two crosses. The cross in the far corner will close the application down and the cross below it will close the file.

PC MASTER TIP

If you still cannot find the program that you want to open, you can search in **My Computer**. There will be a folder in it which has the icon for the program you need. Double click it to open it.

PROGRESS CHECK EXERCISE

Can you open a program using the Start menu?

Try to open WordPad. This is a simple word processor that comes as standard with most computers.

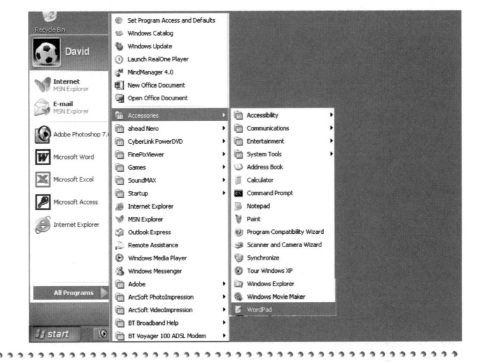

Can you open an application by clicking on a file that you have previously saved?

If you have not saved a file, open an application using the **Start** menu. Then save the file using the **Save** icon.

Now try to find the file. Double click it to open it.

Can you close a file that you are working on without closing the application?

 ## MASTERCLASS

Can you find the icon for an application by clicking on **My Computer** and looking in the folders? Once you have found it, can you create an icon for it? (See page 22)

1001010101101001010010101110101010110101010101101101100001010110

SKILLS

.: Keeping organised :.

It is very important to keep your work well organised so that it is easy to find again. Each document you save is called a **file** and these files can be stored in **folders**. There is usually a folder set up for this purpose on a computer when you buy it. The folder is called **My Documents** or, if there are many users, it has a specific name, e.g. **Rachel's Documents**. It is a good idea to keep all your files in this folder, but you should create new folders within this one to keep your files organised.

.: Naming files :.

This structure is very simple and gives a good starting point when trying to find a file. It is very important to give a file a suitable name so that you can recognise it easily when you see it, but it is also important to plan the names of your folders carefully.

.: Saving files :.

You need to save your work regularly so that you do not lose it if the computer crashes. To do this, click on **File** on the main menu bar and then **Save** or **Save As** if you want to rename the file.

My Documents

File Edit View Favorites Tools Help

Back Search Folders

Address My Documents Go Norton

File and Folder Tasks

Make a new folder
Publish this folder to the Web
Share this folder

Home Folder   My Music   My Photos   My Pictures   School Folder   Rachel's work

PC MASTER TIP

Draw out the structure of your folders before you start saving files so that you can see all the folder names. This will help you to decide where to save a file.

SKILL IN ACTION

Tammy the Teacher keeps her worksheets for different classes in different folders. Pupils at her school are divided into Key Stage 3 (Years 7–9) and Key Stage 4 (Years 10–11). On her computer at home Tammy has set up folders to make it easy to find the worksheets. She carefully planned her folder structure first.

She knows that if she wants to find a worksheet for Year 8 pupils about photosynthesis, she needs to look in her school folder, in Key Stage 3, Year 8, biology and photosynthesis.

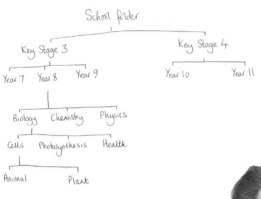

EXERCISE

Can you draw a folder structure similar to mine to keep your files organised?

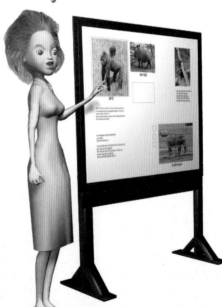

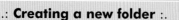

SKILLS

.: **Creating a new folder** :.

You can create a new folder in two ways. For example, if you want to add a new folder in your school folder, open the 'School Folder'. Click on **File** and then **New**. The following menu appears:

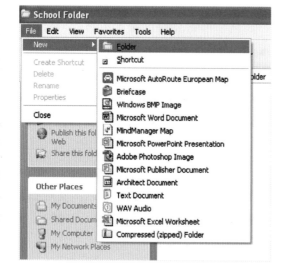

.: **Naming a new folder** :.

Click on **Folder** and a new folder appears. Type in the name of the folder and then press **Return**. If you do not give the folder a name, it will be called **New Folder** as a default name.

.: **Naming a new folder** :.

Occasionally you will want to save a file when there is no suitable folder to save it in. You can also create a new folder by clicking on the **New Folder** button.

You can then name the folder and select it to save the work into this folder.

💡 PC MASTER TIP

Your folders will be shown in alphabetical order. If you want them to appear in a different order, put a number in front of the name, e.g. '1 home folder', '2 work folder', '3 games folder'.

0100100101011010010100101011101001010101011101010110111000101010

 PROGRESS CHECK EXERCISE

Can you create a new folder called 'Home folder' in your documents by using the File button on the menu bar?

Can you save a file into a new folder by using the New Folder button?

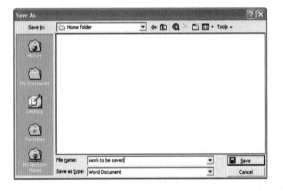

Can you set up a series of folders to keep all your files in?

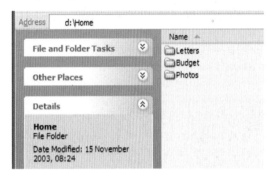

Can you rename an existing folder?

Right click on the folder and select **Rename**.

MASTERCLASS

Can you organise all your files into folders so that they are easy to find?

0100101011010010100101011010010101010111010101101110000101011

SKILLS

.: Keyboard symbols :.

Most of the buttons on the keyboard are self-explanatory: it is very obvious what they do. There are some buttons, however, that need a bit of explanation. Firstly, the symbols. On each of the number keys and symbol keys there are two options because there are more symbols than can fit on a standard keyboard. Some of the less common symbols do not appear on the keyboard at all, but you can access them from a toolbar.

To type the upper character on a button you need to use **Shift**. This is represented by an arrow pointing up.

.: Keyboard symbols :.

If you are using a lot of numbers, you may find it easier to use the keypad on the right-hand side of the keyboard. To type the numbers, make sure that **Number Lock** is on.

To write in capitals, use the **Shift** button and hold it down as you type the letter. If you are using a lot of capitals, you can use the **Caps Lock** button to type only in capitals.

The **Tab** button  is used to move the cursor across the page to set points. This is useful for writing columns of text which all start at the same point.

The **Delete** button will remove the character *after* the cursor. Do not confuse it with the **Backspace** button, which will delete the character *before* it.

PC MASTER TIP

Each function button has a use, as do **Control (Ctrl)** and **Alt**. These are used as shortcuts and you can find out what they do by looking on the drop down menus from toolbars.

SKILL IN ACTION

Sandy the Secretary uses the keyboard to input information on to the computer. She is a touch-typist, which means that she knows where all the keys are, and she can type 60 words a minute without even looking at the keyboard. This is fantastic for typing text, whether in small or capital letters, but she is slowed down dramatically by having to type symbols. When she types up the budget information, she needs to include lots of symbols and a slight error might make a huge difference to the final figures.

	A	B	C
1	Xmas Disco		
2			
3	Costs		
4			
5	DJ	£ 60.00	
6	Sweets	£ 100.00	
7	Drinks	£ 100.00	
8	Hall booking	£ 200.00	
9	Photocopying	£ 20.00	
10			
11	Total cost	£ 480.00	
12			
13			
14	Income		
15			
16	Ticket receipts	£ 180.00	
17	Sweets	£ 180.00	
18	Drinks	£ 190.00	
19			
20	Total Income	£ 550.00	
21			
22	Profit	£ 70.00	
23			
24			

When she is typing a letter, she sends it to her manager to be proofread. The manager often changes her mind and asks Sandy to add sections here and there. Sandy makes sure that **Overwrite** is turned off before she starts typing, so that she does not accidentally go over what she has written.

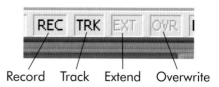

Record   Track   Extend   Overwrite

EXERCISE

Can you write a new sentence in the middle of a paragraph, firstly overwriting a current sentence, then inserting it before a sentence?

J100101011010010100101110100101010101110101010110111000010101011

SKILLS

.: Ctrl and Alt :.

These two buttons work like the Shift button. You hold them down as you press another button and it changes the function of that button. They are normally used to create shortcuts to functions. If you want to make some writing bold, you can either use the button on the toolbar or the shortcut **Ctrl-B**. This means that you hold down the **Ctrl** button while pressing the 'B' button.

Other common shortcuts using **Ctrl** are:
Ctrl-S Saves your work
Ctrl-P Prints your work
Ctrl-U Underlines the selected text
Ctrl-C Copies the selection
Ctrl-V Pastes the selection

Alt is used for accessing the toolbar so that you do not need to use a mouse. If you look at the main menu bar, there is normally one letter in each word underlined.

.: Ctrl and Alt :.

If you hold **Alt** while pressing **F**, the File menu will open. If you then press **S** the file will be saved.

Both these buttons can be held together or with the Shift button to create more functionality. For example, if you want to write the Euro symbol, hold **Ctrl** and **Alt** while pressing the number '4'.

You can also shut down your computer quickly by holding **Ctrl** and **Alt** while pressing the **Delete** button.

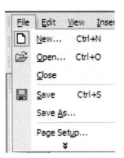

.: Number Lock :.

To use the keypad, press the **Num Lock** button at the top of the keypad. A light will indicate that it is on.

PC MASTER TIP

Once you are familiar with shortcuts, you can use them to speed up commands by using the keyboard rather than the mouse, e.g. holding **Ctrl** while pressing **P** will print the document.

PROGRESS CHECK EXERCISE

Can you write your name with a capital letter at the start of each word?

E.g., Simon Cook

Can you write all your name in capitals by using Caps Lock?

E.g., AIMIE WALKER

Use the keypad to enter a list of numbers into a spreadsheet. Turn off **Num Lock** to see what happens.

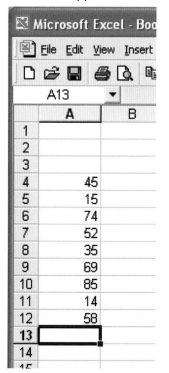

Can you write the following sentence in a word processor *exactly* as it appears here?

"How much?", said John. "I could get a better one for £30.00." Aiysha was not impressed!

Can you write an email address using the '@' symbol?

E.g., mail@lettsed.co.uk

Can you write a 'Euro' symbol (€)? It is found on the same button as '4' and '$'. You will need to be holding down **Ctrl** and **Alt** when you press the button.

E.g., €3.50

Can you move to the previous page or the next page by using the Page Up and Page Down buttons?

 ## MASTERCLASS

Can you learn five keyboard shortcuts and use them to save time when you are writing a letter?

SKILLS

.: Icons :.

It is easier to open a program or file if there is an icon on the desktop. This means that when you turn on the computer, there will be an icon on screen that you can double click on to open up the file or program.

This is useful if you want to leave a file for someone else to find easily or to save time if you use a program regularly.

There will probably already be icons on your desktop when you turn your computer on. These are ones that the supplier of your computer thinks will be useful to you. You can make new icons or delete old ones very easily.

.: Clutter :.

Do not use too many icons. They make the screen look cluttered and they take up memory.

PC MASTER TIP

Decide which icons you really need on your desktop and delete the rest. This will not delete the program and you will be able to get them back later if you change your mind.

SKILL IN ACTION

Dave the Designer saves the files that he is currently working on on his desktop so that he can find them easily.

He deletes the icon once he has finished a project and creates a new icon when he begins a new one.

This is useful because he can see clearly what he is currently working on and he can prioritise his time depending on deadlines.

The programs that Dave uses frequently are also on his desktop as icons. He leaves them there permanently to save time.

EXERCISE

Can you create icons for documents that you are currently working on, perhaps homework files or projects?

0100101011010010100101110100101010101110101011011100001010110

SKILLS

.: Creating an icon :.

To create a new icon right click on the desktop (avoiding existing icons) and a menu appears. Move down to **New** and another menu appears. Click on **Shortcut**.

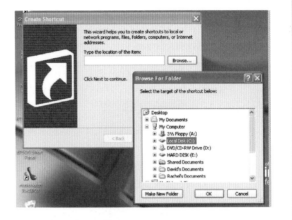

.: Creating an icon :.

A pop-up screen appears asking you to specify the location of the file. Click on **Browse** and then find the file or application that you want to make an icon for.

Click on **Next** and write a suitable name to go under the icon. Finally click on **OK** and the icon will appear on the desktop.

.: Deleting an icon :.

To delete an icon, right click on the icon and move the pointer down to **Delete**. A pop-up message appears to check that you want to delete the icon and to remind you that this will only delete the icon and not the program.

Click **Yes** to delete the icon.

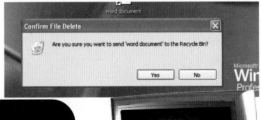

💡 PC MASTER TIP

You can arrange the icons any way you like on the desktop, but you need to make sure that the **Auto Arrange** option is not selected or this will arrange them for you. Check this by right clicking on a blank area of the desktop and selecting **Arrange icons by,** then click to remove the tick by **Auto Arrange**.

PROGRESS CHECK EXERCISE

Can you create an icon for WordPad on your desktop?

You will need to find the file. It is normally located somewhere like 'C:\Program Files\ Windows NT\Accessories'.

Can you create an icon for a Word document?

Can you delete these icons?

Can you arrange the icons so that they line up across the top of the desktop rather than down the side?

 MASTERCLASS

Can you arrange the icons so that similar applications are grouped together?

Office applications

Image applications

Internet applications

Games

SKILLS

.: Burn out :.

Screen savers are designed to stop monitors suffering 'burn out'. Burn out can happen when one part of the screen has been showing for too long. This does not happen so much now that monitors have improved in quality, but most computers use a screen saver when they have not been used for a while. If they remain unused they will normally go on to standby to save power.

The principle of a screen saver is that the image on the screen keeps moving to ensure that each area of the screen changes colour fairly often. Computers usually come with a set of screen savers, but there are many more you can download from the internet.

.: Different types :.

There are basically three types of screen saver. In one, the image moves constantly so that it reaches new parts of the screen. In the second type, the whole screen changes every few seconds. This is a collection of photographs that rotate in order.

In the third type text scrolls across the screen at a different height each time so that all areas are covered.

Amery Hill School

💡 PC MASTER TIP

Some screen savers, for example fish tanks, have a constant border which never changes. This defeats the object of the screen saver as you may still get burn out in these areas. It is only really a problem for older monitors.

SKILL IN ACTION

Vicrum the Vet uses screen savers on his computer partly to protect the monitor, but mainly to give information. He uses the marquee screen saver and changes it daily to show different messages.

The screen saver for the receptionists has a message for them.

Smile :) It's Friday

Screens that customers can see in the practice are used to remind customers about services and important dates.

Don't forget to worm your cats

Vicrum thinks that this is a very good way to give out information and reminders.

EXERCISE

Can you change the settings on the marquee screen saver to give a message to the next user of the computer?

01001010110100101001011101001010101011101010101101110000101011C

SKILLS

.: How to set up a screen saver :.

The screen saver option is in the display option on the control panel. You need to click on the **Start** button and select **Control Panel**. A menu appears showing various options.

Display

.: Settings :.

Double click on **Display** and another menu appears.

Click on the **Screen Saver** tab. Now you can select which screen saver you want. You can also select the length of time before the screen saver switches on. There are more options available by clicking the **Settings** button.

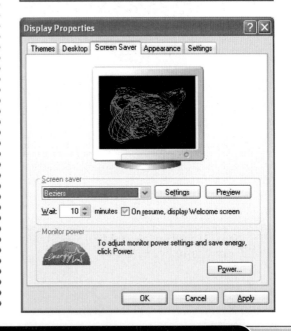

PC MASTER TIP

If you download a screen saver, you first need to copy it into the same folder as the other screen savers. Search for files ending in 'scr' to find where to save the screen saver. (See page 56)

10010010101101001010010111010010101011101010110111000010101

PROGRESS CHECK EXERCISE

Can you change the screen saver to '3D pipes', and set it up so that it comes on after five minutes?

Can you set your screen saver so that it will not come on at all?

Can you set up a 3D text screen saver so that it displays your name after three minutes?

Can you set up a screen saver that will scroll a reminder across the screen?

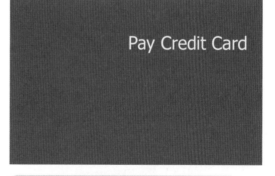

MASTERCLASS

Can you set up a screen saver to display photographs that rotate in order?

SKILLS

.: Protection :.

It is possible to password protect many different areas of your computer to stop people having access to it. You can put a password on the computer itself, so that when the computer is turned on it asks for a password. You can set up your own user area so that a password is needed to get into *your* work, but people can still get into other areas of the computer.

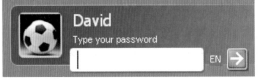

David
Type your password

EN →

.: Screen saver passwords :.

You can also put a password on a screen saver so that if you leave your computer for any length of time, the screen saver comes on and you need to enter the password to get back into your work.

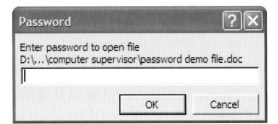

Password [?][X]

Enter password to open file
D:\...\computer supervisor\password demo file.doc

| |

[OK]   [Cancel]

.: File passwords :.

You can put a password on a file so that only you can open that file. You can also password protect parts of files, for example in spreadsheets and databases, so only certain people have access to those areas of the file.

In this section, you will learn how to password protect your user area and a screen saver.

💡 PC MASTER TIP

Remember, the more passwords you use, the more you need to remember. If you password protect an area, you cannot get into it unless you know the password, so take care! Also, never use the same password too many times as people are more likely to see you using it and they will try this first for all your important files!

01001001010110100101001011101001010101011101010110111000010101

 ## SKILL IN ACTION

Donald the Doctor password protects his computer because there is sensitive information on it that no one else should have access to. The Data Protection Act states that 'suitable measures must be taken to keep sensitive information secure', so he must change his password regularly and not let anyone else know it.

Donald also password protects some of his letters so that no one else can see them. Once he has finished a letter, he uses the Options menu in Tools to add a password.

> It is time to change your password.

He also password protects his screen saver so that if he leaves the computer and he is away for a long time he knows that nobody else can get into his computer to see the files.

EXERCISE

Can you think of a series of passwords that you will not forget, to protect your work area?

0100101011010010100101110100101010101101010110111000010101101

SKILLS

.: User password :.

You can set a password to your user area by clicking on the **Start** button and then on **Control Panel**. There is an option called **User Accounts** and, on some computers, **Passwords**. Click on this icon and you can set a password by clicking on the name of the account that you want to change.

Click on the name and a further menu appears.

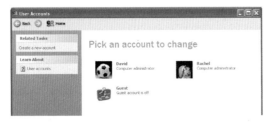

.: Log on :.

Click on **Create a Password** and type your password in twice. When you log on, you will now need to enter the password to get into your user area.

To set a screen saver password, go to the screen saver menu by clicking on **Control Panel** and then **Display**. The **Screen Saver** tab has an option to **Password Protect on Resume**. Tick this box to activate the password.

Your password will be the same as your log on password, so you cannot use this function unless you have a log on password.

PC MASTER TIP

To get a password for a document, use the **Tools** menu on the menu bar and click on **Options** and then **Security**. Here you can set a document password.

10010010101101001010010101110100101010101110101011011100001010

 # PROGRESS CHECK EXERCISE

Can you set a log on password?

Log off and check that your password works.

Without resetting your password, set a screen saver password.

Can you change your password?

It is important to do this regularly as someone might have found out what it is.

 ## MASTERCLASS

Can you set a document password for a word processing document, a spreadsheet and a desktop publishing document?

1101010101101001010010101110101001010101010101110101001011101101100001010101

SKILLS

.: Menu and toolbars :.

There are many functions that a computer can perform. Most of these are used by clicking on buttons on a menu bar or a toolbar. Menu bars and toolbars are usually found at the top or at the bottom of the window and there is usually at least one showing.

```
Document1 - Microsoft Word
File  Edit  View  Insert  Format  Tools  Table  Window  Help
```

.: Table and Borders toolbar :.

One toolbar that you might find useful is the **Tables and Borders** toolbar. This can be used to insert a new table or to adapt one that has already been created. Two useful tools are **Draw** and the **Eraser**.

These can be used to add or remove lines without changing whole rows or columns. You will need to click the buttons again to turn the tools off so that you can use the mouse.

.: Drawing toolbar :.

There are many other toolbars that can be shown when you need them. For example, if you are drawing images on a document, you will want to see the **Drawing** toolbar so that you can have easy access to all of these functions.

Most of the functions on the toolbars are accessible via the main menu bar and the drop down menus, but it is much easier if there is a button to click.

```
Draw ▾  ⇩ ○  AutoShapes ▾  ╲ ╲ □ ○ 🔲 🔳 ◢ 🔞  ◇ ▾ ╱ ▾ ▲ ▾ ≡ ≣ ⇄ ▤ ▯ ▯ ▾
```

.: Other toolbars :.

Some other useful toolbars are the standard **Word** toolbar,

```
□ ☞ 🖫 🔒 ⬛ 🔍 ✓ ✗ ✄ 🗈 ✗ ◁ ▸ ▾ ◁ ▸ ▾ ⬛ 🔲 □ ▦ ⬛ ⬛ ¶ 91% ▾ ⬚ ▾
```

the standard **Excel** toolbar

```
□ ☞ 🖫 🔒 ⬛ 🔍 ✓ ✗ 🗈 🗈 ✗ ◁ ▸ ▾ ◁ ▸ ▾ ⬛ Σ ƒ* ↓A ↓A ⬛ ⬛ 100% ▾ ⬚
```

and the **Formatting** toolbar.

```
Normal  ▾  Times New Roman  ▾ 10  ▾  B  I  U  ≣ ≣ ≣ ≣  ┊≣ ⋮≣ ⟨≣ ⟩≣  ▢ ▾ ╱ ▾ ▲ ▾
```

💡 PC MASTER TIP

Sometimes a toolbar has more buttons than can be shown at one time. If the button you want is missing, look for two small arrows pointing to the right. This will reveal additional buttons.

1001001010101101001010010101110100101010101110101011011100010101

 ## SKILL IN ACTION

Tammy the Teacher often chooses to view extra toolbars because she regularly uses functions that do not appear on the main menu bar. Here are two good examples of this. Firstly, she wants to make a worksheet where pupils type the answers in on a computer, but she wants each answer to be from a selected list. To do this she creates a form in Microsoft® Word and while she is making the document she opts to view the Forms toolbar.

She hides this toolbar when she gives the pupils access to the document and they can only choose from the set answers.

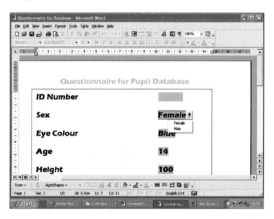

She also does a lot of drawing using vector graphics on some of her worksheets. The easiest way to do this is to view the Drawing toolbar so that the options are always there. This is also useful for drawing text boxes that the pupils can use to label some of the diagrams.

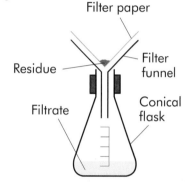

Filter paper

Residue

Filter funnel

Filtrate

Conical flask

EXERCISE

Can you view the **Drawing** and **Forms** toolbar at the same time?

SKILLS

.: Available toolbars :.

There are many toolbars in each type of program which generally work the same way. There is a **View** option on the main menu bar. Click on this and a drop down menu appears. Then move the pointer to **Toolbars** and a list of the available toolbars appears.

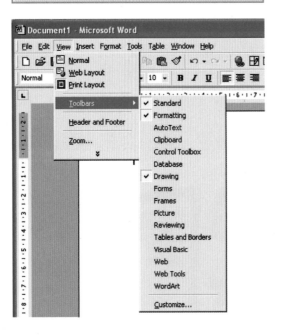

.: Viewing a toolbar :.

The toolbars that are already showing have a tick next to them. To view a new toolbar, click on the name of the toolbar.

If the toolbar is showing, but you cannot see the buttons that you want, find the **Toolbar Options** button.

.: Customising a toolbar :.

If there are no extra buttons available, only the down arrow will show.

You can also customise a toolbar, which means that you can add new buttons to an existing toolbar. This can be useful if you are using **Subscript** and **Superscript** a lot. To do this, go to **View**, select **Toolbars** and click on **Customize** at the bottom of the drop down menu.

PC MASTER TIP

Do not show too many toolbars at the same time as this will drastically reduce the amount of screen space you have available to work in.

PROGRESS CHECK EXERCISE

Can you view all the toolbars available in one application at the same time? (Just to see what is available and to see how the screen space is reduced.)

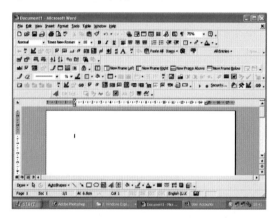

Use the **Toolbar Options** button to see what you can do with the toolbars.

Can you change the way a toolbar appears?

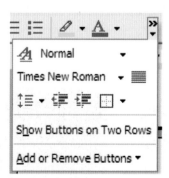

Can you change the order in which the toolbars appear?

You will need to click on the edge of the toolbar without clicking on any buttons.

If you move the toolbar to the side of the window while you are dragging it, you can put the toolbar down the side.

Can you do this and then get it back to the top?

 # MASTERCLASS

Can you add a button to a toolbar? You will need to use the **Customize** option.

SKILLS

.: Display settings :.

After a while, you might find that the colours you have on the screen are not as clear to you as to others. You might also just get bored with the way the computer screen appears. You can alter the appearance of the screen by using the display settings.

You can also buy a desktop theme, or download one from the internet, and use this to liven up your computer screen. Some people change their desktops regularly so that they have a different look every week.

.: Background and fonts :.

The most commonly used part of the display settings is probably the **Background**. This is in the desktop menu. You can select any picture to be the background to your computer screen and really personalise your computer.

There may be writing on your desktop that is too small to see clearly. If so, you can select a larger font from the display settings.

💡 PC MASTER TIP

If your screen looks too large for the monitor, the screen resolution may be wrong. You can correct this by changing the settings.

📁 SKILL IN ACTION

Harry the Hotelier regularly changes the background on his computer screen to show different photographs he has taken with his digital camera. He wants to show the public that the hotel holds functions and conferences as well as having the normal facilities, so he takes photographs around the hotel and changes the background on all the computer screens that are seen by the public.

He also changes the screen saver regularly using the display settings and, as he has one or two staff who prefer larger writing on their desktops, he has set these up with a larger font.

EXERCISE

Can you change the background of your computer screen to a different pattern?

SKILLS

.: Changing the screen :.

All of these options are accessed in the same way. Click on the **Start** button and select **Control Panel**. Double click on the **Display** icon and a menu appears.

By clicking on the tabs at the top of the menu, you can change the menu displayed.

.: Background :.

To alter the background, click on **Desktop** and select a different background from the drop down menu. There is an easy way to place a photograph on your background. Open the photograph, right click on it and select **Set as Desktop Background**.

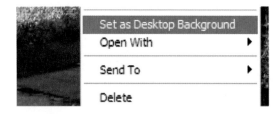

.: Appearance :.

To change the appearance of the windows, click on the **Appearance** tab. You can also alter the font on this menu.

Finally, to change the theme on your desktop, use the **Themes** tab. This will change the standard icons, the pointers and the sounds so that they all follow the same theme.

PC MASTER TIP

There is always a **Default Settings** option, which will restore your settings to the way they were originally if you decide to change your new settings back.

PROGRESS CHECK EXERCISE

Can you change the background of your desktop to a photograph that you have taken?

Can you change the desktop theme of your computer?

Can you change the colours of the windows?

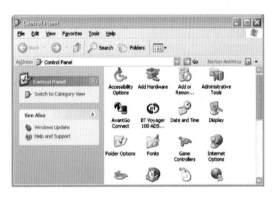

Can you set the writing on the desktop to font size 20?

Size 10

Size 16

Size 20

Size 40

☑ MASTERCLASS

Can you alter the settings of the screen resolution so that the whole screen appears smaller or larger? There will be an optimum setting for your computer which is probably, but not always, the default setting.

0100101010110100100101001011101001010101011101010110110010101011

SKILLS

.: Moving and copying :.

When you are organising your files or just rearranging them within your folders, it is useful to be able to move or copy them. The **Move** option will delete the file from the folder that it was in originally and move it to the new folder. The **Copy** option will copy the file into another folder, so that the file will be in two folders.

If you are simply rearranging the files into different folders, use the **Move** option, otherwise the file will take up twice as much memory because it is saved in two places.

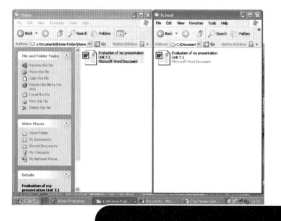

.: Backing up :.

If you are backing up some files, or putting them on floppy disk to transfer them between computers, the best option is to copy them. You will then still have the original copy if you lose or break the floppy disk. Increasingly people are backing up their files on to rewriteable compact disks as these are less likely to get damaged than floppy disks and they hold a lot more information.

.: Removable storage media :.

Memory sticks and card readers are simple to use and plug in to the USB port of a PC. You can copy files on to them and easily transfer them between computers.

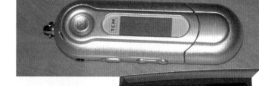

💡 PC MASTER TIP

Some people are afraid to move files in case they lose them. If you are worried, copy the file first, then delete it after you have checked that it has reached its destination.

1001001010110100101001011101001010101110101011011100010101

SKILL IN ACTION

Kate the Kitchen Designer often backs up her work on to CD-ROM in case something goes wrong with her computer. She always saves her work into folders to keep each project separate. When she backs her work up, she copies all these folders into the CD-ROM folder and then clicks on **Write these files to CD**. She has then got a permanent copy of the work in case her computer crashes.

She also needs to copy completed projects on to a disk to show to her customers. She does this by the same process.

Kate does not use the Move function for either of these jobs because she wants to keep the original copy on her computer so that she can still work on it.

When Kate has completed a project to the customer's satisfaction, she moves the file from her PC to a back up disk. That way, she still has the file but it is not taking up space on her computer.

Address | D:\

CD Writing Tasks
- Write these files to CD
- Delete temporary files

File and Folder Tasks
- Make a new folder
- Publish this folder to the Web

Files Ready to Be Written to the CD

Home | Letts | School

EXERCISE

Can you copy some of your files on to floppy disk?

SKILLS

.: Copy and paste :.

The second method is to select the file by clicking on it once in **My Documents** and then pressing **Copy**. You can then open the folder where you want the file to go and press **Paste**. The file will appear in this folder.

The third way to copy or move a file is to select the file by clicking on it once and then click **Edit** on the menu bar. **Move** the pointer down to **Copy to Folder** or **Move to Folder** depending on which you want to do.

You can then browse for the folder you want to copy or move to (or create a new folder) and the file will move there when you click on **OK**.

.: Drag and drop :.

There are many ways to copy files. One way is to have both the folder you are copying from and the folder you are copying to open. Click on the file with the left mouse button and drag it from one folder to the other. Let go of the mouse button and the file will 'drop' into this folder. If you want to move a file by this method, you need to delete the original file afterwards. This will have the same effect.

PC MASTER TIP

To save you having to do them individually, select several files and the computer will copy or move them all at the same time.

01001001010110100101001011101001010101011101010110110001010

 PROGRESS CHECK EXERCISE

Can you copy a file from one folder to another?

Can you copy one folder into another folder?

Can you move a file from one folder to another?

Can you copy and paste a file into a different folder using the toolbars and then delete the file from the original folder?

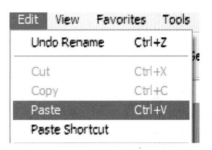

Can you use the Copy to Folder method to copy a file from 'My Documents' into a new folder called 'Personal stuff'?

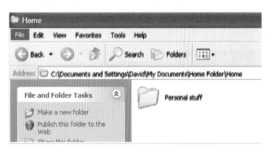

 MASTERCLASS

Can you copy five files in a folder into another folder all in one go? This is the same as moving it.

SKILLS

.: Adding programs :.

Most computers already have a lot of software installed but you may not have all the programs that you want. You may have bought some more and want to install them. This is getting easier as computers become more user-friendly.

The first experience that most people have of installing software on to a computer is a computer game, and this is exactly the same process as installing an application for work. Most CD-ROMs now come with autoplay set up so that the CD runs automatically. This will often automatically start the installer that sets the application up.

.: Installing/uninstalling :.

To install the software, follow the instructions on the screen. You will often be asked to restart the computer as some changes have been made that will only activate once the computer starts up. Once you have done this, you are ready to go.

Some programs do not start up automatically. In this case you need to find the **setup.exe** or **install.exe** file.

To uninstall some software, you need to find the **Add or Remove Programs** icon in the control panel. Double click on this, and find the software you want to uninstall. Click on the name of the software and follow the instructions to remove the program from the computer.

Add or
Remove
Programs

 PC MASTER TIP

It is always better to uninstall software rather than delete it as there may be some system files saved in other places that will also be removed. You might miss these if you were deleting the files by hand.

1010010101101010010101001011101010011011100001010

SKILL IN ACTION

Sue the Scientist is always finding new software to put on her computer as there are programs being developed all the time. She checks that the software is compatible for her computer by reading the minimum specifications required to run it.

Windows 2000 Professional
- Intel Pentium (or compatible) 133MHz or higher processor
- 64 MB of RAM

Windows Me
- Intel Pentium (or compatible) 150MHz or higher processor
- 32 MB of RAM

Windows 98
- Intel Pentium (or compatible) 133MHz or higher processor
- 32 MB of RAM

REQUIRED FOR ALL INSTALLATIONS
- 70 MB of available hard disk space
- DVD or CD-ROM drive
- Internet Explorer (minimum version 5.0 required, 5.5 recommended)

Email scanning supported for standard POP3 and SMTP compatible email clients.

Supported instant messenger clients:
- AOL® Instant Messenger 4.7 or higher
- Yahoo!® Instant Messenger 5.0 or higher
- MSN® Messenger and Windows® Messenger 4.6 or higher

Once she has checked that the program will run on her computer, she buys it. She puts the disk into her computer and waits to see if it will run automatically. New programs usually do. She installs the program to her 'Program Files' folder and creates an icon to go on the desktop.

She can then run the program.

If after a while she decides that the program is not really as useful as she had thought it would be, she can uninstall it to free up more space on her computer.

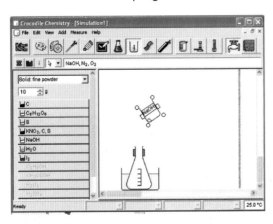

EXERCISE

Check the specifications of your computer so that you know whether or not a game will run on it.

1010010101101001010010111010010101011101010110111000010101

SKILLS

.: Automatic :.

If a program starts to install automatically, you just follow the on screen instructions. If it does not start automatically, then you need to find the install file. This will be on the CD-ROM (or floppy disk). To run the file, click on the **Start** button and then **Run**.

.: Run 'box' :.

Click on the **Browse** button and then select the CD-ROM or floppy disk. This will show the files on the disk. Find the file called '**setup.exe**' or '**install.exe**'. Double click on this and it will put the file name in the Run 'box'.

Click on **Run** and the program will start to install.

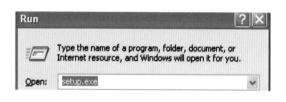

.: Add and remove :.

Another way to do this is to click on the **Start** button, then open **Control Panel**. Double click the **Add or Remove Programs** icon, click the **Add New Programs** button on the left-hand side and then follow the on screen instructions.

To uninstall a program, start in the same way but click on the file to uninstall. Follow the on screen instructions and the program will be removed from your computer.

 PC MASTER TIP

Do not delete programs that you have never heard of. Some of them work behind the scenes to make the computer work more efficiently. The simple rule is not to delete any application that you are not sure about.

100100101011010010100101110100101010101110101011011000010101

 PROGRESS CHECK EXERCISE

Can you install a computer game on your computer?

Can you install a program without using autoplay?

To do this, you might need to leave the CD-ROM in the drive and exit the install menu. This cancels the automatic installation so that you need to install the program manually.

Can you create icons for new software that you have installed?

Can you uninstall a program that you have just installed?

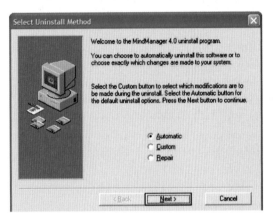

You do not need to actually do this. You can begin to uninstall the program, then cancel uninstall before you get to the stage where files are being deleted.

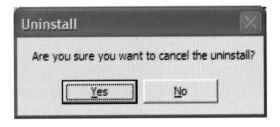

 MASTERCLASS

Can you look at the specifications of a computer program in a shop and be sure that it will run on your system?

01001010110100010100101011101001010010101110101010110111000010101100

SKILLS

.: Two windows :.

It is useful to have two windows open at the same time because you can then work on two files. Perhaps you are copying sentences from one file to another or researching in one window and writing your document in the other.

It is also possible to have three or four windows open but if you open any more than that, the windows become too small to see properly.

.: Dragging :.

It is also useful to be able to drag information from one window to the other.

Most people only work with one window at a time, but it can be a nuisance having to minimise a window in order to see a second.

If you are not careful, you might remove the file from the original folder. Always check both folders after moving or copying a file.

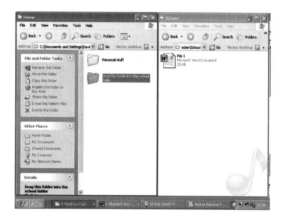

PC MASTER TIP

If you need two windows fully open you can switch between them by holding down the **Alt** button and pressing **Tab**.

SKILL IN ACTION

Sophie the Student often has two programs running at the same time. She does a lot of research on the internet and needs to include information she finds in her word processing document.

She wants to look up some current weather information for her geography project and finds a good website at www.itv.com/weather. She does not need all the information on the page. She just wants some data about the local area to include in her document.

It is easier to keep the web page open, open the word processing document and then transfer the information from the website to her document.

EXERCISE

Can you open your web browser and a word processor at the same time and transfer information from a web page to a document?

SKILLS

.: Minimise, maximise, close :.

At the top right-hand side of the window there are three buttons.

The **Restore** and **Maximise** buttons are never shown together. The **Maximise** button is replaced by the **Restore** button when a window is maximised (full size).

Minimise   Maximise   Close   Restore

.: Opening two windows :.

Make sure that the **Maximise** button is showing, (i.e. you have selected **Restore**), then you will be able to alter the size of the window by moving the pointer to the edges, clicking and then dragging. Make the window cover exactly half the screen in this way, then make another window to take up the other half. You can now see both windows at the same time.

PC MASTER TIP

You can still use all the same functions in each window. You may need to zoom out so that you can see more of the page.

01001001010101101001010010101101001010101011010101011011000010101

 PROGRESS CHECK EXERCISE

Can you open two word documents at the same time?

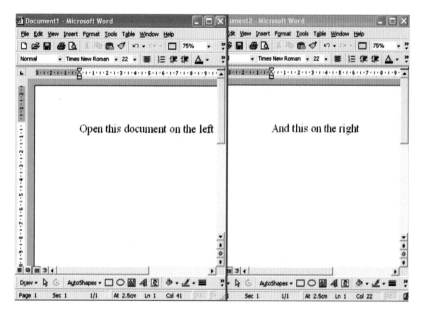

Can you open a web page in your web browser and a word document at the same time?

SKILLS

.: Checking date and time :.

On many documents, it is possible to add the date and time automatically. It is therefore important that it is correct.

The time is permanently displayed in the bottom right-hand corner of the screen, so it is easy to check it. To check the date, move the pointer over the time and the date will appear.

.: Time zones :.

If you are producing a document that has many drafts, it is useful to put the date on, and sometimes the time, so that you know quickly which is the latest copy. By inserting the date as the current date, you will not need to change it on the file. The current date will be automatically inserted, as long as the date on your computer is set up correctly.

It is also possible to set up the time zone so that the clocks go backward and forward automatically.

PC MASTER TIP

The clock on the computer runs off a battery inside the PC. It will not need resetting, even if you have left the computer off for a long time.

SKILL IN ACTION

It is very important to Harry the Hotelier that the clocks are set correctly on his computers for a number of reasons.

The date is automatically inserted on to his customer's bills and if this is incorrect, it looks unprofessional and could lead to confusion.

The wake-up call system is linked to the computers. When a customer wants to be woken at a certain time, the computer calls their phone number. If the time is incorrect, this will result in some very unhappy customers.

It is also useful for Harry to be able to check the time when calling hotels around the world. That way he can avoid telephoning at inconvenient times.

EXERCISE

Can you insert the time on a document that will change automatically?

SKILLS

.: Time menu :.

The easiest way to change the date and time is to double click with the left mouse button on the time in the bottom right-hand corner of the screen. This will produce a menu.

You can click on a date to change it and type in a new time below the clock to alter the time.

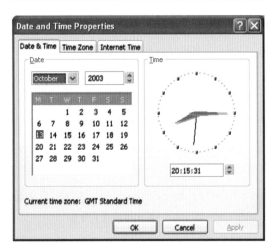

.: Add the current date and time :.

To add the date and time to a Word document click on the **Start** button and select **Control panel**. Double click on the icon for **Date and Time** to see the same menu.

To add the current date or time to a document click on **Insert** on the main menu bar and move the pointer down the drop down menu to **Date and Time**. From this menu select the format that you want to appear on the page, click on it and it will show the current time.

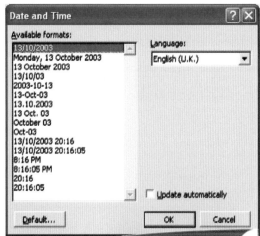

💡 PC MASTER TIP

It is assumed that if you are going to put the date or time on a page it will either be at the top or the bottom. For this reason, when you add a header or footer, the date and time options show as buttons on the toolbar that appears.

PROGRESS CHECK EXERCISE

Can you set the time of your computer to exactly six o'clock?

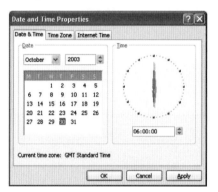

Can you set the date so that it reads October 13th?

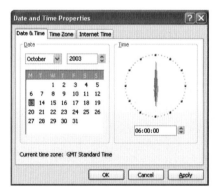

Can you insert a date on a document in Microsoft Word so that it always shows the current date?

Can you insert a date on a Microsoft Excel Spreadsheet so that it appears in the header?

Click on **View**, then **Header and Footer**. The following menu appears:

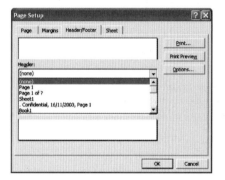

Either select one of the default options or click on **Custom Toolbar**. Then click on the **Insert Date** button.

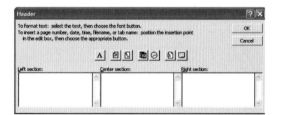

 # MASTERCLASS

Can you set up a document so that the current date appears in the middle of a sentence?

SKILLS

.: Search function :.

Occasionally, you will need to look for a file because you are not sure where you saved it. If you have a good file and folder structure and some idea where the file is, you can search by clicking on the folders and try to find it by chance.

There is a better way. As long as you have some idea what the file is called, you can search for it using the **Search** function. This will search for a file name or part of a file name in the directories or drives where you think the file could be.

.: * symbol :.

You can search for part of a name by using the * symbol to represent the missing text. For example, if you know you want to search for any Microsoft® Word file, you can search for *.doc. This will list all the Word files.

💡 PC MASTER TIP

You can set up the search so that it will only look in certain areas of the computer. If you search the whole computer, it could take several minutes.

SKILL IN ACTION

Tammy the Teacher regularly needs to search for files as there are some files that she only uses once a year and she forgets where she has saved them. She wants to find a worksheet containing data about the weather. She knows that it was an Excel document and that it was called something like 'downloaded data' or 'weather data'.

She does a search on *data*.xls in her **My Documents** folder. This means that there can be any characters before and after the word 'data' and the file must end in .xls.

She finds a number of Excel files that include the word 'data' and can quickly see the one she wants.

EXERCISE

Try to search for a file using the * symbol to represent some letters.

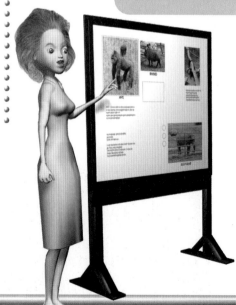

010010101101001010010101101001010010101101010110110110000101011C

SKILLS

.: Search menu :.

Click on the **Start** button and then click on **Search** to bring up the Search menu.

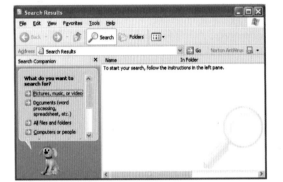

.: Advanced options :.

Now click on the type of file that you are searching for. This helps the computer to narrow down the search. The computer then asks you for the date of the file or to exclude some dates from the search, again, to narrow down the options. If you click on **Advanced Options**, the computer will give you the choice of drives to search.

.: Results list :.

The results are shown in a list. To open a file, double click on it with the left mouse button or just make a note of the folder that it is in.

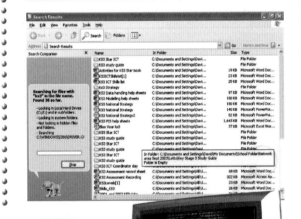

PC MASTER TIP

Always start your search by being as specific as possible. If the file you want is not there, you can make the search more general later.

PROGRESS CHECK EXERCISE

Can you search for the file that runs MS Paint?

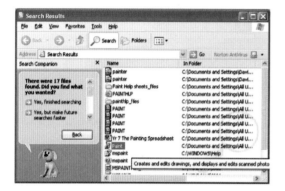

Can you search for a file of any type containing the word 'window'?

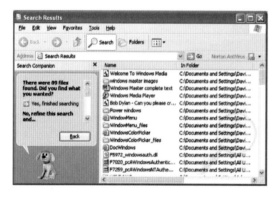

Can you list all the Word documents on your computer?

Can you find where all the different fonts are stored on your computer?

You will need to search for Truetype font files (ending in .ttf).

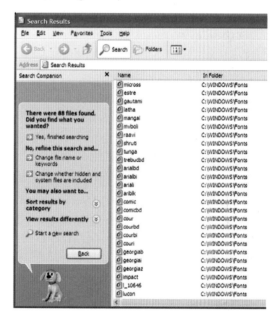

This is useful if you download a new font and want to know where to save it.

 ## MASTERCLASS

Can you create a search that will look for all Microsoft® applications?

SKILLS

.: Find :.

It is useful to be able to search a large document for a specific word. You might want to change a phrase or find out where a certain paragraph is. There is a function on the word processor that allows you to search for a word. There are similar functions in other applications, for example on Internet Explorer there is a **Find on this page** option.

It is also possible to bring up this menu by using a shortcut. This is done by holding **Ctrl** while clicking on **F**.

.: Replace :.

When you have found your word, you may find that you have spelled it incorrectly throughout the document. You can use the **Find and Replace** tool to correct all the spellings. This is useful if the spellchecker has not picked up the errors.

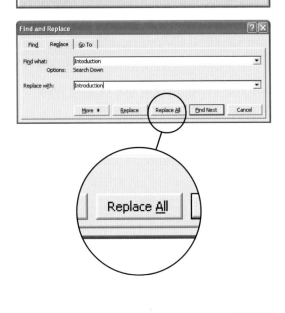

PC MASTER TIP

Be careful when replacing small words. If you replace 'car' with the word 'coach' all the way through a document, it will also replace the 'car' in 'careful' to make the word 'coachful'.

SKILL IN ACTION

Sophie the Student often uses the internet to research information for her assignments. Once she has found the website that she wants, she likes to go straight to the relevant section. The fastest way that she has found to do this on large documents is to use the Find on this page option.

She is looking for information about Martin Luther King and in particular his famous speech. She goes to a search engine first and searches for "Martin Luther King".

When she finds a suitable website, she uses the Find on this page option and searches for the word 'speech'.

If this is not the correct reference, she can use Find Next to find the next time the word appears. This really helps to speed up her search.

EXERCISE

Can you find a site about Martin Luther King and find the word 'speech' on that site?

10010101101001010010111010010101011101010110111000010101101

SKILLS

.: Find option :.

The Find option is normally found in the drop down menu from **Edit** on the main menu. Click on **Edit**, then move the pointer down to **Find**. The following menu appears:

Find and Replace dialog box:
```
Find and Replace                    [?][X]
 Find | Replace | Go To
Find what: [                    ▼]
    Options: Search Down

              More ▼  [Find Next] [Cancel]
```

.: First reference :.

Type the word that you are looking for and press **Enter**. The computer searches the document for the word you want and highlights the first reference.

After studying Arthur Miller's play, *The Crucible*, I have come to the conclusion that the three people most to blame for the witch hysteria and the subsequent death of innocent people are _____, and _____. Each of these people, in some way, caused harm to blameless people and I will in this essay explain what these people, knowingly or unknowingly did to...
in 16...

BO

FIR

```
Find and Replace                    [?][X]
 Find | Replace | Go To
Find what: [crucible              ▼]
    Options: Search Down

              More ▼  [Find Next] [Cancel]
```

.: Replace tab :.

If this is not the word that you want, click on **Find Next**. This will find the next time that the word appears.

If you click on the **Replace** tab, the menu is slightly different.

```
Find and Replace                    [?][X]
 Find | Replace | Go To
Find what: [crucible              ▼]
    Options: Search Down
Replace with: [                  ▼]

        More ▼ [Replace] [Replace All] [Find Next] [Cancel]
```

.: Replace all :.

You can now type in what you want to replace the word with. For example, if you have spelled 'Amery' as 'Amrey' all the way through the document, you can replace them all simply by clicking on **Replace All**.

```
Find and Replace                    [?][X]
 Find | Replace | Go To
Find what: [Amrey               ▼]
    Options: Search Down
Replace with: [Amery            ▼]

        More ▼ [Replace] [Replace All] [Find Next] [Cancel]
```

 PC MASTER TIP

You do not have to search for a whole word, you can type a few letters and the computer can search for them.

PROGRESS CHECK EXERCISE

Can you search a Word document for a specific word?

Can you count how many times you use the word 'the' in a document?

You will need to use Find Next to go from one to the next.

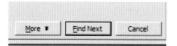

Can you replace all the 'offs' so that they are spelled correctly?

Write a document and deliberately spell the word 'of' as 'off'.

Can you search a website about sharks for the word 'fin'?

The death of whale shark "The harmless giant" caused by human greatly disturbs the world's divers and naturists. Continual illegal hunting of whale sharks for ■■s and meats are reported in the territorial waters of some countries in both South Asia and South East Asia of more than 1000 whale sharks killed offshore.

This crisis shows signs of slowly moving toward Thai territorial waters.

Can you find a specific number on a spreadsheet in Microsoft Excel?

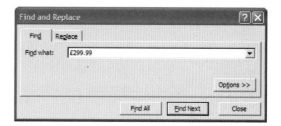

This can be very useful if you want to keep track of your spending on a spreadsheet.

✓ **MASTERCLASS**

Can you use **Find and Replace** to change an article written in the first person to one written in the third person?

SKILLS

.: Start menu :.

The Start menu is what appears when you click on the **Start** button.

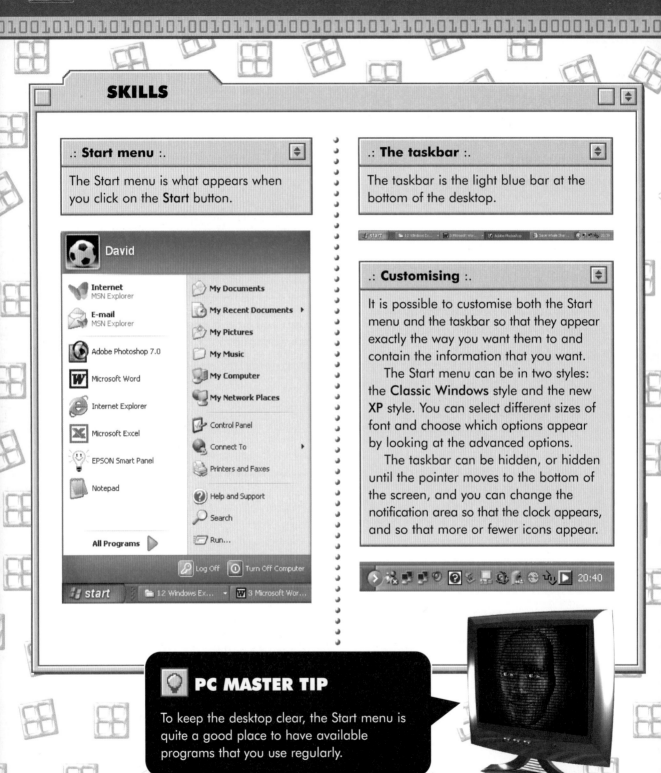

David

Internet
MSN Explorer

E-mail
MSN Explorer

Adobe Photoshop 7.0

Microsoft Word

Internet Explorer

Microsoft Excel

EPSON Smart Panel

Notepad

My Documents

My Recent Documents ▶

My Pictures

My Music

My Computer

My Network Places

Control Panel

Connect To ▶

Printers and Faxes

Help and Support

Search

Run...

All Programs ▷

Log Off | Turn Off Computer

start | 12 Windows Ex... ▾ | 3 Microsoft Wor...

.: The taskbar :.

The taskbar is the light blue bar at the bottom of the desktop.

.: Customising :.

It is possible to customise both the Start menu and the taskbar so that they appear exactly the way you want them to and contain the information that you want.

The Start menu can be in two styles: the **Classic Windows** style and the new **XP** style. You can select different sizes of font and choose which options appear by looking at the advanced options.

The taskbar can be hidden, or hidden until the pointer moves to the bottom of the screen, and you can change the notification area so that the clock appears, and so that more or fewer icons appear.

20:40

💡 PC MASTER TIP

To keep the desktop clear, the Start menu is quite a good place to have available programs that you use regularly.

1001001010101101001010010101101001010101011101010101101011000010101

SKILL IN ACTION

Neville the Newsagent has the taskbar hidden on his computer so that his customers cannot see what programs he has open when they are at the till.

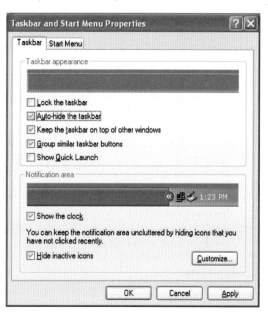

His shop can be quiet for long periods so if there is no shelf stacking or administration work to do, he passes the time playing computer games.

His customers might think this is rather unprofessional but once he has read all the papers, the day can get quite boring. He never neglects a customer and always minimises the game when someone walks into the shop, but he feels happier that the computer is set up to hide the files that he has open on the shop computer.

EXERCISE

Can you hide the taskbar so that the open programs are not shown?

010010101101001010010111010010101011101010110111000010101101

SKILLS

.: Start menu options :.

To access the Start menu options click on the **Start** button, then on **Control Panel**. To open the menu, double click on the **Taskbar and Start Menu** icon.

Taskbar and Start Menu

When opened the menu has two tabs at the top, one is the **Start Menu** options, the other is the **Taskbar** options. The Start Menu has two options, the **Classic Windows** start menu or the **XP** start menu. You can customise each one to change the contents.

The options are all on this menu. There are more options in the **Advanced** tab and they are all self-explanatory.

Customize Start Menu [?][X]

General | Advanced

Select an icon size for programs

⊙ **Large icons**   ○ **Small icons**

Programs

The Start menu contains shortcuts to the programs you use most often. Clearing the list of shortcuts does not delete the programs.

Number of programs on Start menu: 6

[Clear List]

Show on Start menu

☑ Internet: MSN Explorer

☑ E-mail: MSN Explorer

.: Taskbar options :.

The taskbar options are shown in the menu below.

There are further options for customising the notification area (where the clock is). You can select which icons appear there.

Taskbar and Start Menu Properties [?][X]

Taskbar | Start Menu

Taskbar appearance

🔳 start   2 Internet...   📁 Folder

☐ Lock the taskbar
☐ Auto-hide the taskbar
☑ Keep the taskbar on top of other windows
☑ Group similar taskbar buttons
☐ Show Quick Launch

Notification area

« 🖳 🗐 1:23 PM

☑ Show the clock

You can keep the notification area uncluttered by hiding icons that you have not clicked recently.

☑ Hide inactive icons   [Customize...]

💡 PC MASTER TIP

You can move the taskbar to the side or the top of the screen by clicking on an unused area of it and dragging it.

PROGRESS CHECK EXERCISE

Can you set the Start menu so that it has large icons?

Can you set the taskbar so that it is automatically hidden when not in use?

Can you set the Start menu so that ten programs are shown?

Can you move the taskbar to the left of the screen?

✓ MASTERCLASS

Can you set up the taskbar so that it only appears when you move the pointer close to the bottom of the screen?

SKILLS

.: WordPad :.

WordPad is a simple word processor that is supplied free with most computers. It is useful to know how it works because files written in WordPad can easily be transferred between different types of computer. The file is saved as a 'Rich Text Format' file, which has the ending .rtf. This file can only be used for straightforward text, for example, letters and assignments and cannot incorporate images or tables.

.: Word wrap :.

The style of the program is very similar to Microsoft® Word but some of the options are different. One of the options that can be changed is called 'Word wrap'. This is the way in which writing moves on to the next line. You can choose whether the type moves down, on to the next line, when a certain line length is reached, or whether it continues in one long line.

Programmers who write web pages in HTML often use WordPad. It is simple to use where the appearance of the text is not important.

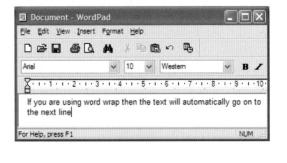

🔆 PC MASTER TIP

If you have a word processor like Microsoft® Word, you can write the text in this software and then convert it so that the text will transfer like a WordPad file.

10010010101101001010010101110100101010101110101010110110001010

SKILL IN ACTION

Donald the Doctor uses WordPad to write his notes at work. He then emails the notes home where he has a computer that uses a different word processor. This means that his notes can be written up at home or at work, and can be read by both word processors.

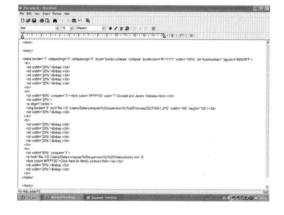

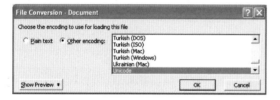

Donald also has a website that he writes as a hobby. He is learning HTML, a computer programming language. He types the instructions into WordPad and then saves the file as an HTML file. He can then open the file using Internet Explorer and view the file as a web page.

Donald and Jane's

Website

Click here for our Dorset photos

Click here for the latest news on the family

EXERCISE

Can you write a letter in WordPad and then open it in another word processor?

1001010110100101001011101001010101011101010110111000010101 10

SKILLS

.: Open WordPad :.

To open WordPad, you need to use the **Start** button and select **All Programs**. Select the folder called **Accessories** and move the pointer to **WordPad**.

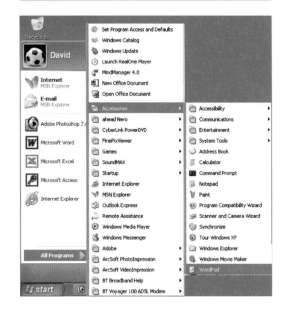

.: Options menu :.

To use WordPad, just type what you need. Most of the options on the toolbar are similar to those in Word. The only different options are those that deal with the way the information is saved and how the text wraps. This is changed by clicking on the **View** button on the main menu bar and then selecting **Options** on the drop down menu.

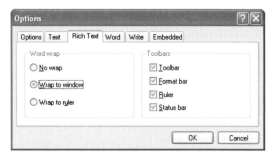

.: Saving :.

When you save a document, if you want to save the font and formatting, you should save the file as a 'Rich Text Format' file (.rtf). Otherwise you can save it as a text file (.txt).

 PC MASTER TIP

There is nothing you can do in WordPad that you cannot do in Microsoft® Word but the files in WordPad generally take up less memory.

1001001010110100101001011101001010101110101011011100001010

 PROGRESS CHECK EXERCISE

Can you make a poster in WordPad?

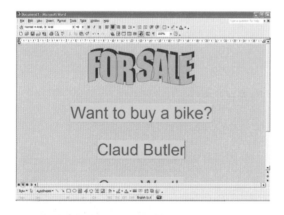

Can you convert the poster into a Word document?

You can then adapt the poster, written originally in WordPad, to make it look more professional.

Can you set up Word wrap so that the text carries on along one line?

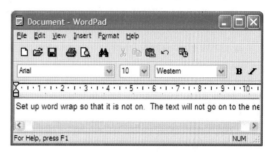

Can you set up Word wrap so that each line ends at the edge of the window?

 MASTERCLASS

Can you save a WordPad file as a .txt file?

0100101010110100101010010101110100101010101011101010101101110000101010110

SKILLS

.: Windows Media Player :.

Most computers have an application that can play music. In the majority of cases, the default player is called Windows Media Player, although you can download other music players from the internet.

There are two types of music file normally used by computers: one is a wav file and the other is an mp3. The wav file takes up a lot more memory and if you download a CD on to your computer, this is the type of file it will be saved as. An mp3 is a more compressed file and takes up less memory, but both files play equally well on Windows Media Player.

.: CD-ROM :.

You can also play a CD directly on your computer using the CD-ROM drive.

.: Visuals :.

The Windows Media player has different 'skins'. Skins change the appearance of the player. You can also set the visualisation so that certain patterns appear on the screen in time with the music. This can be a set pattern or you can arrange it randomly.

PC MASTER TIP

It is important to realise that copying music is illegal. There are plenty of songs on the internet that you can download legally where the artist has given permission. You can also play CDs that you have bought.

SKILL IN ACTION

Sophie the Student plays a lot of music on her computer because it saves her having to have a stereo in her room. Most of the music she plays is directly from CDs. She puts a CD into the computer and it automatically starts Windows Media Player. She can control the volume from the computer screen and from the speakers.

She also downloads songs from free mp3 websites. She likes to listen to new music and when she finds a band that she likes she can go and buy a CD by them.

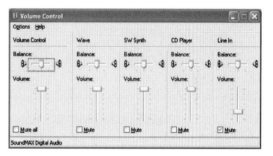

EXERCISE

Can you find a free mp3 website on the internet and play some music?

SKILLS

.: mp3 format :.

Finding a website with copyright free mp3s is fairly easy. There are many new bands that are promoting themselves by releasing free music on the internet and there are some bands that are now selling songs to be downloaded. These files will probably come in mp3 format. You will need to use a search engine to find free mp3s.

.: Playlist :.

You can select music files to play in a certain order so that only the tracks you want are played. This is called a playlist.
You can also minimise Windows Media Player so that it fits on the toolbar.

.: Browse and play :.

You can open Windows Media Player by clicking on the **Start** menu and then **All Programs**. Move the pointer to **Windows Media Player** and the program opens. You can then browse your music files to find a file to play.
If you put a CD in the drive, a menu will pop up asking if you want to play the CD. This is the easiest way to play a music CD.

PC MASTER TIP

Most other music players have the same functions as Windows Media Player. You can download some from the internet as a demonstration and can buy the program if you think it is better than Media Player.

PROGRESS CHECK EXERCISE

Can you play a CD on your computer?

Can you change the skin and visualisation of your music player so that it looks more up to date?

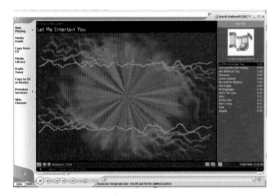

Can you download some free mp3s from the internet and play them?

Can you convert files from a CD to become mp3 files on your computer?

Look at the difference in file size!

Can you set up a playlist from mp3 files?

Let Me Entertain You	5:55
Let Love Be Your Energy	4:44
We Will Rock You	1:19
Monsoon	5:09
Come Undone	5:34
Me And My Monkey	7:20
Hot Fudge	5:45
Mr Bojangles	5:25
She's The One	5:43
Kids	7:21
Better Man	2:11
Nan's Song	4:51
Feel	5:17
Angels	5:55

 MASTERCLASS

Can you convert an mp3 file to a wav file? You might need to download a new media player to do this.

SKILLS

.: Adding a printer :.

A peripheral is any device that is not actually needed for a computer to work, but can be added to increase the number of jobs that a computer can do. The most common peripheral is a printer. This is used as an output device that will print what you see on the screen on to paper. Before buying a printer, you need to consider what you want it to do. Do you need to print in colour? Are you printing a lot of pages? What quality of print do you require? This will help you to decide which printer to get.

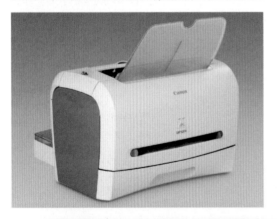

.: Adding a scanner :.

Another peripheral that you might need is a scanner. This is an input device that can copy an image from paper on to a computer. When buying a scanner, you should consider the quality and speed you need. You can also add a digital camera, a personal digital assistant (pda), a fax machine, graphics tablet or barcode reader. They are all installed in a similar way.

PC MASTER TIP

Before you buy any peripherals, check that you have space to plug them in to the back of your computer. Most peripherals can be bought with a USB connection so check that you have enough of these.

SKILL IN ACTION

Ahmed the Artist has just bought a scanner and a digital camera for his computer. He has produced many paintings and wants to save them on to his computer so that he can use them in a book that he is writing. He decides to get an A3 scanner as most of his paintings are slightly larger than A4, and he buys a digital camera to capture images of his larger paintings.

Both the scanner and the digital camera have USB connections.

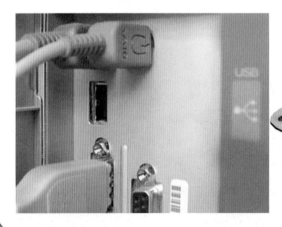

Carefully following the instructions in the 'Quick start' guide, he turns on the computer before plugging in the USB connector. Once he plugs in the scanner, the computer recognises that some new hardware has been plugged in.

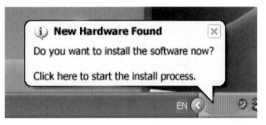

(i) **New Hardware Found**
Do you want to install the software now?
Click here to start the install process.

He follows the on screen instructions and installs the scanner. He repeats the process for the digital camera.

EXERCISE

Can you find out how many USB ports there are on your computer?

SKILLS

.: Adding hardware :.

Read the manual carefully as different devices are installed in different ways. Generally, when you plug in a new device, the computer will recognise it automatically. If it does not, check that it is plugged in properly and start the **Install Wizard** manually. To do this, click on the **Start** button, then on **Control Panel** and finally **Add Hardware**.

Add Hardware

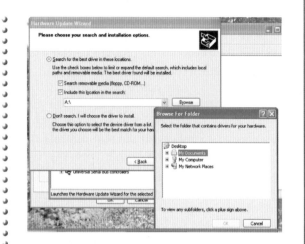

.: Wizard :.

This starts the 'wizard', which helps you to configure the peripheral properly. You will have received a disk with the hardware which contains the files that are needed for the computer to recognise it correctly. When you reach the question about drivers, make sure the disk is in and browse the disk for the driver folder.

.: Wizard :.

As soon as you have installed the device, check that it works. You will normally receive some software with the device to make it easier to use. You should install this as well, but check that you have not already got a better program.

Some peripherals require you to restart the computer in order to change some settings. Make sure that you will not lose any files before shutting down.

 PC MASTER TIP

Check whether you need to run the CD-ROM first. This might tell you when to plug in the device and install any software.

PROGRESS CHECK EXERCISE

Can you identify how many peripherals you can install on your computer?

Decide which peripherals you will really use. Put them in to order of importance and then decide which you need to buy first. Could you get a combination device that has lots of functions, e.g. scanner/printer/fax machine or do you have enough space to have separate devices?

Can you manually start the Add Hardware Wizard?

Can you install a printer on to your computer?

 MASTERCLASS

Try to find the drivers for your printer on the internet and see if there are any updates to improve the performance of the printer.

1100101011010010100101011010010101010111010101101111000010101011 0

SKILLS

.: Saving disk space :.

It is important to delete files from your computer regularly. If you save every piece of work that you do without deleting old files, then the hard drive will fill up very quickly.

You may not want to lose a file permanently, in which case, copy it on to a disk before deleting it. Some files will fit on a floppy disk but it is better to put them on a CD-R or CD-RW as they are less likely to get damaged. They can also hold a lot more information than a floppy disk. If you are sure that it will be of no further use, delete it.

The computer will ask whether you are certain that you are deleting the correct file or folder. If you are, click **Yes**.

Confirm Folder Delete

Are you sure you want to remove the folder 'stone' and move all its contents to the Recycle Bin?

[Yes]   [No]

.: Recycle bin :.

There is one further backup in case you have made a mistake. Files are not lost from the computer when deleted but sent to the **Recycle Bin**. You can restore them from here as long as you do it within a couple of days of deleting the file.

.: Multiple delete :.

You can delete as many files as you want at one time. First, select all the ones to be deleted. The computer will not be specific about the files to be deleted. It will just say **Do you want to delete these 3 files?**

💡 PC MASTER TIP

Most files only take up a small amount of memory. If you have a CD writer, back them up on to CD in case you change your mind and need them in the future.

SKILL IN ACTION

Kate the Kitchen Designer often has to backup her files and delete them from her computer as they are very memory intensive. Each project has a lot of images and once she has finished the project she does not really need them.

She does not want to lose the projects in case another client wants to do something similar with their kitchen. She could show them a previous design from a stored file and adapt the kitchen to suit them.

Every month, Kate copies all completed projects on to a CD-R to back them up. She checks that they have copied correctly by opening them and then she deletes the files from her computer.

She keeps these CD-Rs in a safe place and saves a lot of space on her computer.

EXERCISE

Can you create a backup copy of files that you no longer need and delete the files from your computer?

1100101011010010100101110100101010101110101011011100001010110

SKILLS

.: Delete a single file :.

To delete a single file or folder click once on the relevant icon with the left mouse button and it will be highlighted. Press the **Delete** button on the keyboard (not Backspace) and there will be a message asking you to confirm that you really want to delete this file. Press **Yes** and the file is sent to the Recycle Bin.

.: Multiple delete and restore :.

To delete a number of files at one time, select them by clicking or dragging the pointer over them all. Press **Delete** or choose **Delete** from the **Edit** menu on the main menu bar. The computer will ask you to confirm that you want to delete all these files.

To restore files from the Recycle Bin, right click on the **Recycle Bin** icon on the desktop. Click on **Explore**. All the files recently deleted will be shown. Click on the file that you want to restore and then go to the main menu bar. Click on **File** and then on **Restore** and the file will be returned to the folder it was deleted from.

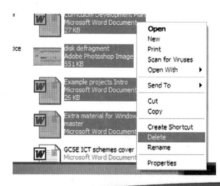

PC MASTER TIP

To delete several files that are not next to each other, hold down **Ctrl** as you click on each file. The previously selected files will remain selected as you click on each new one.

1001001010110100101001011101001010101011101010110111000010101010

 PROGRESS CHECK EXERCISE

Save a blank file in My Documents and call it 'delete me'. Can you delete the file?

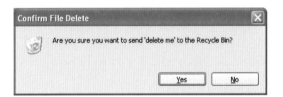

Once you have deleted it, can you restore it again?

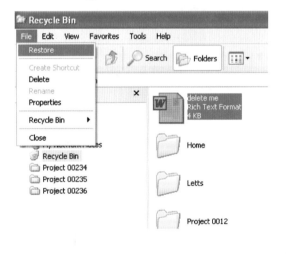

Can you select a number of files to be deleted using the Ctrl button?

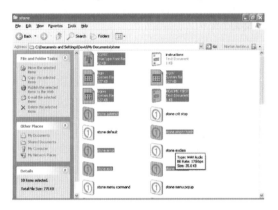

Can you tell if the Recycle Bin has any files in it?

Can you empty the Recycle Bin?

MASTERCLASS

Save several files on to a disk. Can you delete them from your computer and then restore them from your backup disk?

01001010101101001010010101110100101010101011101010110110000101011 0

SKILLS

.: Paint :.

Paint is the most basic drawing package that comes with a computer. It is very easy to use but does not produce as professional a result as other drawing packages. It is excellent for producing simple images. Paint uses bitmapped graphics which means every dot on the picture can be altered.

.: Planning your picture :.

You can plan your picture first by colouring in squares on paper to see how best to draw it on a computer.

Once you have chosen the colours and shapes, you can start to draw it on screen.

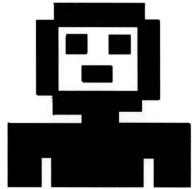

.: Paint tools :.

There are many tools that you can use to adapt your picture and lots of different ways to colour it in. It is best to learn how to do this by experimenting with the buttons and seeing what they will do.

💡 PC MASTER TIP

Be careful not to enlarge a Paint document too much as it will become pixelated, which means that it will start to blur.

1001001010101101001010010101101101001010101011011010101101101100001010

SKILL IN ACTION

Tammy the Teacher uses Paint to draw images for her worksheets. She is creating a worksheet about computers but cannot find the exact image she wants in clipart. She plans on graph paper how to draw the image and then draws it on the computer.

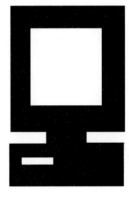

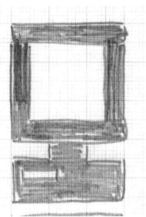

Using this method she can create any image that she wants. She also uses Paint to copy images that she has downloaded from the internet. She can then adapt them exactly the way she wants.

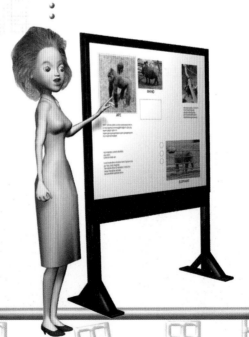

EXERCISE

Can you draw a computer in Paint?

010010101011010010100101011101001010101011101010110111000010101100

SKILLS

.: Using Paint tools :.

Drawing in Paint is very simple once you are familiar with the tools.

This tool selects an irregular shaped area that you decide on by clicking on the mouse whenever you reach a corner.

This tool selects a regular shaped area.

Once you have selected an area, you can colour it in using the **Fill** command or other tools.

.: Other tools :.

The **Eraser** will remove colour as you click and drag it.

The **Fill** tool will fill a selected area or shape with colour.

The **Pipette** selects a colour for colour matching.

The **Pencil** tool draws a pencil line in any selected colour.

The **Brush** tool draws a brush stroke when you click and drag it.

The **Airbrush** tool simulates the effect of an airbrush.

There are more tools but these should be enough to start with.

PC MASTER TIP

The further you zoom in on an image, the more precise you can be with the tools to perfect your image.

PROGRESS CHECK EXERCISE

Can you draw an animal in Paint?

Can you draw the outline of a shape and then colour it in?

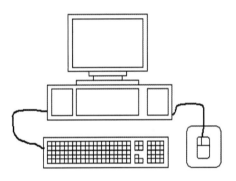

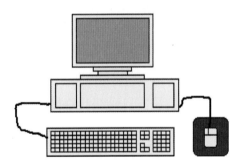

Can you download an image from the internet and adapt it?

Can you change the colours?

 ## MASTERCLASS

Can you draw the design of a building on graph paper and then draw it to the same proportions in Paint?

01001010101101001010010110100010101011101010110101100010101 0

SKILLS

.: Speeding up :.

If your computer runs too slowly, there are a number of things you can do to speed it up. This is often caused by too many programs being open at the same time. By closing some of them down you will speed up the computer.

If this does not work, or you do not have many programs open, try emptying the Recycle Bin.

Recycle Bin

.: Speeding up :.

The next thing to try is to clear the temporary internet files and remove the cookies. These are files that websites use to make them seem more personal. For instance, the website might add your name or save your details on your computer for future access.

Temporary Internet files

Pages you view on the Internet are stored in a special folder for quick viewing later.

[Delete Cookies...] [Delete Files...] [Settings...]

.: Cleaning up :.

In the control panel there are administrative tools that can check the performance of the machine. One of the options is to 'defragment' the hard disk. This means that all the files for one program are sorted so that they are saved together on the hard disk. This will save time when moving between them.

There are other clean up tools that will help to speed up your computer. Some of these can be downloaded from the internet, others you can buy from computer stores.

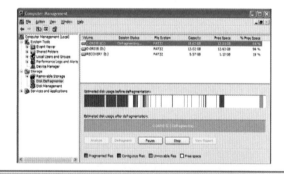

PC MASTER TIP

The computer may also run too slowly if the hard disk is almost full. Check if there is any space left on the hard drive and delete some files if necessary.

`100100101011010010100101011010010101010111010101101100001010`

📁 SKILL IN ACTION

Max the Marketing Executive needs his computer to be running at top speed as he often uses it to make presentations. If it starts to run slowly, he checks whether there are any icons or files that can be deleted.

Once he has done this, he empties the Recycle Bin and clears the internet history and the temporary internet files.

His computer runs his presentations better now but he feels that if he defragged his hard drive, it might improve it further.

Max's computer now runs really quickly.

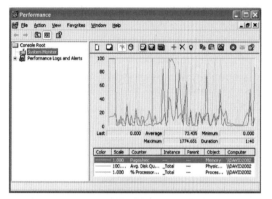

EXERCISE

Can you clear your computer's Recycle Bin?

0100101011010010100101110100101010101110101011011100001010110

SKILLS

.: Empty the Recycle Bin :.

Firstly, move all unwanted files to the Recycle Bin. Right click on the **Recycle Bin** and a menu appears. Move the pointer to **Empty Recycle Bin** and if you are sure that you have not deleted any files that you may need, confirm that you want to empty the Recycle Bin.

Confirm Multiple File Delete

Are you sure you want to delete these 12 items?

Yes   No

.: Clear temporary internet files :.

To clear the temporary internet folders, right click on the **Internet Explorer** icon and move the pointer, on the menu that appears, to **Internet Properties**.

On the next menu, go to the section **Temporary Internet Files** and click on **Delete Files**. When asked to confirm if you want to delete all off line content, click on **OK**.

Delete Files

Delete all files in the Temporary Internet Files

You can also delete all your offline content stored locally.

☐ Delete all offline content

OK   Cancel

.: Defragment the hard disk :.

To defragment your hard disk, you need to click on the **Start** button and then **Control Panel**. Select **Administration Tools** and then **Computer Management**. You can now choose to defragment the disk.

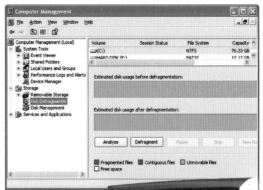

 PC MASTER TIP

Avoid defragging your disk just before you need to use it. It can take a long time and will slow the computer down.

PROGRESS CHECK EXERCISE

Can you empty your Recycle Bin?

Can you clear the temporary internet folder and set it so that less memory is used with temporary internet files?

Can you defragment your disk so that all the programs on the computer are saved in the same area?

Can you set the internet history so that it saves web pages for a shorter time?

Can you monitor the performance of your computer using the Performance check tool in the control panel?

✓ MASTERCLASS

Can you improve the performance of your computer by using the tools provided with the PC?

SKILLS

.: Regional settings :.

Once you have set the time and date, you can select how you want them to appear in a document by looking at the **Regional settings**. The time can be displayed in either the 12 hour clock, with or without A.M. and P.M., or the 24 hour clock.

The date can appear in a number of formats.

10/10/03

could also be written as

10th October 2003

or

10/10/2003

Regional and Language Options

These can all be set from the **Regional settings** menu.

.: Alter language :.

You can also alter the language. This is useful as many words are spelt differently in American English. Your spellchecker will work in the language that you have specified in the Regional settings.

💡 PC MASTER TIP

It is also possible to set the currency so that it appears automatically with a '£' or '$' sign and to two decimal places.

SKILL IN ACTION

Harry the Hotelier makes sure that the Regional settings on his computer are exactly how he wants them so that there is no confusion for his staff. He often has foreign staff working at the hotel to gain experience in using English. This also benefits Harry as they can talk to his foreign customers in their own language. The staff are not always aware that some American English words are spelt differently. If the computer is set up correctly, they can be confident that they have got it right.

Harry has also made sure that the clocks, dates and currency settings are correct so when the bills are printed they look exactly the way he wants them. He prefers the date in the form DD/MM/YYYY and the time to be HH:MM. All currency is set to two decimal places and has a '£' sign.

EXERCISE

Can you set the language so that the spellchecker highlights American English spellings but does not highlight British ones?

The person who designed this poster is French. She can quickly see that she has spelt the word 'coloring' incorrectly.

01001010101101001010010101110100101010101110101010110110000101011C

SKILLS

.: Regional settings :.

The Regional settings can be found in the Control Panel. This is accessed by clicking on the **Start** button, moving the pointer to **Control Panel** and then clicking with the left mouse button.

One of the icons in the Control Panel menu is the **Regional and Language Options** icon. Double click on this with the left mouse button and the following menu appears:

.: Language options :.

This menu is used to change the way that the time, date, currency and numbers appear on your computer. To look at the language options, click on the **Languages** tab. When a menu appears, click on **Details** to change the language option.

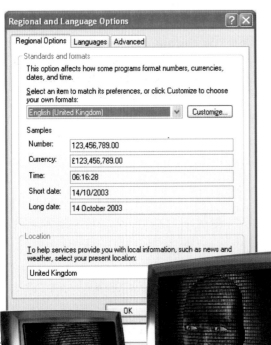

PC MASTER TIP

You can also change the language for a specific document by looking on the **Tools** option on the main toolbar in that document.

PROGRESS CHECK EXERCISE

Can you change the time so that it appears with A.M. or P.M. after it?

E.g., 11:20 A.M.

Can you change the date so that it appears as a long date?

E.g., 11th August 2003

Can you change the language of one document?

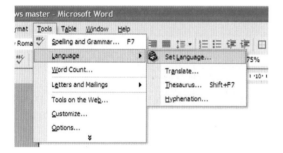

Choose the required language.

Can you find out which language keyboard you are using by looking in the language options?

Can you change the input language to US English? Check that it has worked by writing a Word document with American spellings in it.

E.g.,   center
      color
      gray

 MASTERCLASS

Can you download a new language from your Windows disk by clicking on Add in the language options?

Inter

The Language of Speech and Writing

'A lively and accessible introductory textbook.'

Paul Simpson, *Queen's University Belfast*

'An excellent introduction, well organised, accessible and readable. The book covers the central issues in this important (and developing) subject area.'

Lelsey Milroy, *University of Michigan*

'. . . a clear and readable introduction, with modern, wide-ranging and thorough examples . . . Academically rigorous and thought-provoking.'

Margaret Walker, *Chief Examiner for English Literature A-Level*

This accessible satellite textbook in the Routledge INTERTEXT series is unique in offering students hands-on practical experience of textual analysis focused on speech and writing. Written in a clear, user-friendly style, it combines practical activities with texts, accompanied by commentaries and suggestions for further study. It can be used individually or in conjunction with the series core textbook, *Working with Texts: A core introduction to language analysis*.

Aimed at A- and AS-Level and beginning undergraduate students, *The Language of Speech and Writing*:

- analyses the processes involved in writing and speaking
- highlights the differences between these two modes of communication
- explores written texts including the language of recipes, literary discourse, legalese
- explores spoken texts including: personal chat, telephone conversations, interviews, television programmes
- explores mixed-mode texts including: email, advertisements, written conversations, non-interactive speech
- compares and contrasts spoken and written texts on the same theme.

Sandra Cornbleet is a part-time Lecturer at Nottingham University and Examiner for various English Language examination boards.

Ronald Carter is Professor of Modern English Language at Nottingham University and author of numerous books in the area of applied linguistics. He is also involved in developing the CANCODE project, which is a corpus of five million words of spoken English transcribed and stored computationally.

The Intertext series

◎   Why does the phrase 'spinning a yarn' refer both to using language and making cloth?

◎   What might a piece of literary writing have in common with an advert or a note from the milkman?

◎   What aspects of language are important to understand when analysing texts?

The Routledge INTERTEXT series aims to develop readers' understanding of how texts work. It does this by showing some of the designs and patterns in the language from which they are made, by placing texts within the contexts in which they occur, and by exploring relationships between them.

The series consists of a foundation text, *Working with Texts: A core introduction to language analysis*, which looks at language aspects essential for the analysis of texts, and a range of satellite texts. These apply aspects of language to a particular topic area in more detail. They complement the core text and can also be used alone, providing the user has the foundation skills furnished by the core text.

Benefits of using this series:

◎   **Unique** – written by a team of respected teachers and practitioners whose ideas and activities have also been trialled independently

◎   **Multi-disciplinary** – provides a foundation for the analysis of texts, supporting students who want to achieve a detailed focus on language

◎   **Accessible** – no previous knowledge of language analysis is assumed, just an interest in language use

◎   **Comprehensive** – wide coverage of different genres: literary texts, notes, memos, signs, advertisements, leaflets, speeches, conversation

◎   **Student-friendly** – contains suggestions for further reading; activities relating to texts studied; commentaries after activities; key terms highlighted and an index of terms